COWBOYS

A Vanishing World

PHOTOGRAPHS BY
JON NICHOLSON

MACMILLAN

First published 2001 by Macmillan
an imprint of Pan Macmillan Ltd
Pan Macmillan, 20 New Wharf Road, London N1 9RR
Basingstoke and Oxford
Associated companies throughout the world
www.panmacmillan.com

ISBN 0 333 90208 4

1 3 5 7 9 8 6 4 2

A CIP catalogue record for this book is available
from the British Library.

Designed by Macmillan General Books Design Department
Printed and bound in the United Kingdom by The Bath Press

I went west with an ambition, but very soon my ambition changed. It became my mission to document the great American tradition as a dying breed, struggling to cope with the advances of the twenty-first century. I have been privileged to be close at hand to witness the ways of the West and in these pictures I have simply tried to show how cowboys work and try to understand what they are fighting about. In doing so I have made new friends, friends that must continue to fight for the preservation of their culture, a way of life that most only dream about.

I would like to thank all of them for giving me a part of their lives and for their hospitality. There are too many to list in full, but there are two men and their families without whom I would not have had any direction, Les Davis, of the CS Ranch in New Mexico and his family, and James Owens, of Clarendon, Texas. James in particular brought me back down to earth with his knowledge and his ability to ply me with endless cups of coffee to fight the jet-lag. I only discovered years later that it was decaf.

And a special thanks to Jack and Lindy Craft, Jeff Haley, and Jim Owens, Randy Davis, and Beau and Kathleen White, and Ian Dickens and Sara Cubitt at Olympus Cameras.

I give this book to my family: Molly, Maisy, Sam and my wife Emma.
Thank you all for letting me go on this Journey.

bulls and to keep out of their thunderous way when they were thrown off. Here I listened to the stories of the contractors who supplied the bulls, hearing how they'd adapted to the rigours of the new century, men with unshakable belief in tradition coupled with great faith in the future.

It hadn't taken me long to realize that the reality of the cowboy world is a far cry from its celluloid version and the way of this perennial American icon is struggling to establish its place in the new millennium. The backdrop has changed: the grand vistas of the open range have been ploughed up by the Interstates; the countryside is being devoured by the Walmart phenomenon; the vast empty skies are crisscrossed by miles of high-tension cable, supported by huge ungainly pylons.

On another occasion, as I looked over the red rock of the Palu Duro Canyon, deep in the Texas Panhandle, and watched the cotton-wool clouds slowly drift high above the parched pastures, a fine red dust billowed up from the ground. It found its way into my eyes and nose, and under my shirt, and into my camera. This dust is part of a story only too well known in most parts of the West. To cattlemen and cowboys, grass is crucial to their way of life. It is lush green pastures fed by rain that give the cows their essential weight. But this dust cloud was a symptom of an eight-year drought that has held west Texas and New Mexico in its fierce grip. It has sucked dry the towns of Reserve and Datil and is reaching up north into the shadow of the Sangre de Cristo mountains of New Mexico. Without life-giving rain, and with grazing land eaten up steadily by the urban sprawl, cattlemen are being forced into the unemployment queues. While the physical landscape and environment has changed, there is also a human threat to the way of the cowboy: government bureaucracy is chipping away at the backbone of the American dream and ranchers now must cope with a society and culture that encroaches on their fragile exisitence.

There is a ranch in northern Arizona where a family has lived and worked for five generations. Originally they drove their herd of cattle from Oregon, bringing with them the logs to build a new home and a new life. But permits to the land they have leased have been refused, and they are now no longer allowed access to water their cattle. Father and son have been reduced

AKA Ranch, near Datil, New Mexico.

to smashing the rocks on the very land they worked and loved, driving the load to Phoenix and selling it as building materials. In this case, as in so many, the bureaucrats have won. In ranches all over the West, cattlemen are fighting to keep their land against fierce opposition; opposition that carries with it the extra weight of an official stamp.

From the movies to music, from the catwalk to commercials, the cowboy is an icon with many faces.

But in my journey to discover the way of the ranch community, I was shown the flipside of the myth. Old West historians, friendly waitresses and ranchers themselves gladly offered their advice and wisdom. They told me who to speak to, which libraries to visit and even the history to study. Because, as James Cattron, of Cattron County, New Mexico, told me, to fully comprehend the West today, you must first understand the past. He instructed me to delve into my own history to the understand the problems of the present. And, as I did this, my romantic notions of life on the open range soon evaporated into the harsh realities of American rural life.

For centuries the herdsmen of Scotland, Ireland and Wales have traded and worked with each other. Many Scots emigrated from the Hebrides and the lowlands of Scotland to the more fertile pastures of Ulster and many of them were caught up and killed in the fighting that erupted in the 1640s. The English influence in Ireland threatened many of them with poverty and ruin. Their options were few. Many chose to migrate once more and ended their torturous journeys in the Southern states of the USA and Virginia. There they established new lives, maintaining many of the traditions of their homelands. These Celts were known for their riotous behaviour; they were called Crackers or Rednecks or even White Trash. And as such they soon began to long for the isolation of the plains. They pushed west, going back to the fundamental way of life they'd known for generations. They herded their sheep and cattle, just as the Vaqueros had driven their cattle from Mexico to America in the late 1500s.

Now their journey has come full circle. The 'Absentee Landlord' of government bureaucracy is once again forcing the cowboys from their land, pushing them away from the land that their forefathers made home.

Red Rock Canyon, Sedona, Arizona.

Nick, Oscar and Lilly Aucker. Davis Camp, Palu Duro, Texas.

Icke Roberts. Marathon, Texas.

Willy Wetherton, fencer. Clarendon, Texas.

Glen Souza. Haleakala Ranch, Maui, Hawaii.

Rodeo. Laughlin, Nevada.

Jack Craft. Adrian, Texas.

Jeff Haley. Oaks Creek, Texas.

Rhett Cauble. JA Ranch, Palu Duro Canyon, Texas.

Rhett Cauble.

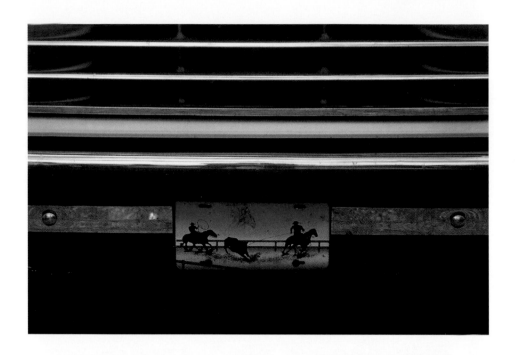

Tombstone, Arizona.

Water tank. Texas.

The General. CS Ranch, New Mexico.

Branding. Kenton, Oklahoma.

BRANDING

Two men stand by their pick-ups, their horses gently scraping the bottom of the trailer: the day has begun. The light in the yard is still grey, the sun isn't high enough yet to illuminate the white buildings of the CS Ranch in Cimarron, New Mexico. The tangy aroma of hot coffee comes mixed with the smell of freshly made breakfast burritos. Foil wrappers crunching and the vigorous splash of the last dregs of coffee in the dust show that it is time to leave HQ.

It's the first branding of the year, a time to see if the hands will remember the tricks of roping, of doctoring a calf; will remember how to keep the irons hot but not too hot – just enough to give an even burn. There's a nervous anxiety in the cab of the pick-up with the new irons in the back. Unanswered questions float in the air. Who should rope first? Which crew should work the left side? Should they use three crews? Friends, family, even the police chief have taken a day off to work the three hundred head. There are even two guys from Louisiana who came on vacation to a neighbouring ranch some years back and now make an annual trip to help brand.

In the cab the heater is blasting out hot dry air, some-thing is stuck in one of the vents, making a continual clicking sound, while the radio announcer witters endlessly about some aspect of the latest presidential embarrassment. The two men share a wry laugh.

'Looks like wind's gotten up. Have to watch the fire, put her close to the fence . . . what ya think?'

'Think Dad'll want his chair same place as last year?'

It went on.

We pull off the road, through the gate and down the track to the corral. Large wooden fences seem to be placed randomly but as we come close it becomes clear that they mark out six pens. The wood is dry and grey from years of wind and rain passing down from the mountains of Colorado south-eastward onto Clayton and into the panhandles of Texas and Oklahoma. But today the sky is almost blue, and a rich golden light hangs parallel to the ground.

The two men have grown to six or maybe eight. Saddles are tightened, extra jackets are put on, gloves pulled over cracked and scarred hands. One hand holds a small knife, whipping it on the leather chap of the left leg, leaving a rough patch in the leather.

Les Davis, family owner of the CS Cattle Company. Cimarron, New Mexico.

'Sharp 'nough to work.'

The six or eight has grown to maybe twelve, young and old, man and wife.

Groups pass boxes of syringes, vaccination bottles, a chair for Dad to sit in and cast his experienced eye across the corral from where he can see whether the ways of branding passed to him years back are still in the heads of his pupils. And then the irons, six of them, and the large gas cylinder and rack which has now taken the place of the open fire are put into position. The group divides itself into teams, friendships are rekindled, jokes flow but all minds are firmly on the job in hand. Younger members watch, learning, working when directed, mainly talking about college and graduation.

The time has come, time to bring in the cattle. Horses and their riders gather at one corner of the long rectangular corral. A voice calls out, directing the riders over the vast pasture beyond.

'Bring 'em up slow, Dave, you and Jack pull 'em up through the draw and along the fence . . .'

'We'll get in here then split 'em up, put them calves in the next pen, split 'em in two or three groups, work 'em and on to the next pen.'

One man remains to move everything into position, making sure that the fire is close to the fence, that Dad's chair is placed right where he can see all three crews working. Before the hour is up the faint sound of cattle can be heard on the wind, which blows twirls of dust across the work area. The man by the fire leans his shoulder into each gust, the brim of his hat fluttering slightly as the wind lifts it.

'Gonna have 'ta keep an eye on this son of a gun t'day. 'S gonna keep goin' out in this here wind.'

The cattle are now close to the corral, cowboys and cattle all moving at the same speed into the entrance. By now the group has swollen to twenty, kicking up a thick cloud of red-brown dust. Some of the riders aren't here to work but to witness the first branding of the year on the CS. It is 7.30 a.m.

In amongst the dust cloud shouts and whistles can be heard as two hands split up the groups of cows and calves, fifty to each pen, with six pens in all. Eventually they are ready to brand, with two men mounted in each

CS ranch hands.

Randy Davis, putting the finishing touches to a new branding iron.

crew, seven others on hand to hold the animals, inject them and leave the brand on the hindquarters of the calves. Nerves have turned to excitement as the first group enter the corral, horse and riders swinging through the group of young calves. One rider flicks his rope over the head of a calf and with a flick of the wrist directs the rope under the animal, pulling it tight around the hind legs. A roar and claps from the onlookers and a smile from Dad as the first calf is dragged through the dust towards the crew.

The calf is rolled over and the team moves in. Castration and inoculations take minutes. A cry and a cloud of smoke come from the calf as the brand comes down on its flanks. The streams of fresh blood running in the earth show how many calves have been worked.

The riders become more and more confident with their roping, the onlookers more vocal in their disapproval of a missed opportunity. Slowly the dust shifts away as the cattle are led out to the pasture, calves almost tripping their mothers in their desperation for a reassuring suckle.

The cowboys lead their horses into a large circle. The pick-up rolls slowly over the rutted ground, pulling a trailer of feed for the herd. One man pulls his gloves back on and with his knife cleanly slices the line holding the bails together and starts pushing them off the back of the trailer.

At 11.30 the onlookers start to disperse, leaving the dirty-faced workers anticipating lunch.

Kim, Dad's daughter, serves up lunch at her ranch house down the road. Men and women sit and eat.

'Sure tastes good, Kim.'

'Why, thank you . . . have some more.'

'I'll be seein' you all, then.'

'Work's not gonna git done sittin' here.'

'Thanks for helpin' out, Charlie.'

The screen door slams on the porch and the rumble of the pick-ups can be heard as the crews return home. The sun is now beating down hard on the white buildings, swallows fly in and out of their nests under the roofs and doorways; horses roll lazily in the hot dust, easing the itch of the saddles before joining the rest of the herd, head to wind, eyes closed. The group of twenty has returned to two.

Their work finished, they too go their separate ways to other tasks that the hot afternoon has in store.

Below Wheeler Peak.

Randy Davis (centre) riding out to gather cattle for branding.

Dave Kennecke.

Roping on the CS.

First branding of the year.

Dinner. Kenton, Oklahoma.

Dragging and flanking a calf.

Branding. Bell Ranch, New Mexico.

Cimarron River, Kenton, Oklahoma.

Maui, Hawaii.

After a hot morning on Oaks Creek Ranch, Texas.

Jim Ferguson. Kenton, Oklahoma.

At 10.00 a.m. the temperature was into the upper 90s. Oaks Creek Ranch, Texas.

Jack Craft holding the rope tight, awaiting its release during a late branding.

Ferguson Ranch, near Black Mesa, Kenton, Oklahoma.

Mothers and their calves are reunited. CS Ranch, Cimarron, New Mexico.

Katie Cotter. Odessa, Texas.

James Owens, boot shop. Clarendon, Texas.

James, who passed away Christmas 1999, was the man who put me straight on the core point of my project. He was the centre of a small community, his name and the legend of the boots he made is known all over the world. His son Jim carries the flame.

Rhett Cauble. JA Ranch, Texas.

JA saddle room. Texas.

Casper, Wyoming.

Route 66, Arizona.

Boot shop. Clarendon, Texas.

Amarillo, Texas.

Stockyards. Amarillo, Texas.

Cattlemen at the Amarillo stockyards.

Look behind you!

cowboy on the TV screen, rather than the reality of a life of hardship. He now saves all his money and spends his allocated visa time travelling around the States riding bulls.

Our final evening before I dropped him off to get his plane on to the next leg of this particular trip was in Lubbock, Texas. A guy who teaches rodeo to young kids had offered him a few free rides.

The last ride of the day looked as if it was going to get the better of him. The bull was going beserk trying to unseat him. The gate flew open and off they went, Jean clinging on and a ring of clapping and cheering circling the arena. This was all a little premature, as the bull suddenly pulled up and stood stock-still in the middle of the arena. Silence. Jean, who is over six foot, was almost standing although still astride the bull.

A young kid ran out from the fence and gently prodded the bull with a stick. This was the red rag it needed, it arched its back and took off with Jean looking like a permanent fixture. Unfortunately for Jean the bull came back to earth whilst Jean was heading for a spell on the Mir space station. Silence once more, and then an enormous thud as Jean reconnected with terra firma.

He had nevertheless won the affection of this small group of Texans.

Jean and Loy Davis. Texas.

Jean. Odessa, Texas.

Jean. Lubbock, Texas.

Singing 'The Star-Spangled Banner'.

Shaking a margarita.

In the boot shop, Texas.

Monument Valley, home to John Ford's epic Western, *Stagecoach*. Utah–Arizona border.

On Highway 70. The gate to Johnny Hill's place, near Clarendon, Texas.

Gold under the ground. A well near Valentine, Big Bend of Texas.

Billy Klapper, spur maker. Pampa, Texas.

Spurs. The Western Heritage show, Abilene, Texas.

Chilean spurs.

"HOPE"
CATTLE PRICES
WILL RISE
AGAIN

Bunkhouse. Wyoming.

Stockyards. Amarillo, Texas.

Oaks Creek Ranch, just following a storm which put down a tornado. Texas Panhandle.

Andy. Haleakala Ranch, Maui, Hawaii.

Jim Owen. Clarendon, Texas.

Jason and James Gardner. Lysite, Wyoming.

Story-telling. Evetts Haley Library, Midland, Texas.

Visitors donating memorabilia to the Evetts Haley Library.

Barry Clower. Texas.

Jack Craft. Texas.

Mario Marther. Big Bend, Texas.

Mario marther, Tx.   1/2000

Cimarron, New Mexico.

RODEO, THE MAVERICK CLUB

Fifty prominent members of the village of Cimarron, New Mexico, created the Maverick Club in August 1922. With social, civic and educational objects as its purpose, it avoided political and religious viewpoints. The name 'Maverick' was adopted to denote a group of strays that neither the Rotary, nor the Kiwanis, nor the Lions could welcome under their rules, yet that had a desire to follow similar objectives. There are no dues for membership, and once a man is invited to join the club he is a member for life. On 4 July 1923 the newly formed Maverick Club sponsored a rodeo for the community, which has become an annual event and a contest with the Raton Rotary Club.

During the subsequent seventy-three years, the exploits of members of the Maverick Club have been many and legendary. In the early 1990s the back meeting room at the St James Hotel was dedicated as the new Maverick Room. The past president, Rod Taylor, saw it fitting to keep up with the bullet-hole-ridden walls of the previous Maverick Room by pulling out of his belt an old Brinley Colt .44, pulling the trigger and blasting a hole into the wall.

Later in the same decade the outgoing president Barney Coppedge refused to give up the reigns to incoming president Charles Duran at the 1998 Ladies night. Charles shot Barney. The 1998 Rodeo also ended an eighty-eight-day drought with a downpour. The entire second half of the rodeo was a mud bath for contestants and onlookers alike.

The wild tradition of the Maverick Club continues into the last rodeo of the 1900s. It draws people from Texas and Oklahoma and north from Colorado. It's a great family day out, but keep one eye looking over your shoulder for somebody wanting to have a little fun.

Fourth of July Rodeo. Cimarron.

Carr Vincent.

End of the day.

Laughlin, Nevada.

Cimarron, New Mexico.

Abilene, Texas.

Cimarron, New Mexico.

Western Heritage Show. Abilene, Texas.

Dos Amigos Rodeo Arena, Odessa, Texas.

Prayer before rodeo. Farmington, New Mexico.

The kid on the left would not leave me alone and kept bumping me, so I told him to go away, then he walked into and made this shot. Lubbock, Texas.

Rodeo. Farmington, New Mexico.

Abilene, Texas.

Rodeo ground. Lubbock, Texas.

Abilene, Texas.

Roping. The pot of gold at the end of the rainbow. Maui, Hawaii.

Roping practice. Maui, Hawaii.

Rodeo, Abilene, Texas.

Entering Dos Amigos Rodeo. Odessa, Texas.

Pool at the Dos Amigos.

Rodeo. Odessa, Texas.

Mutton-busting.

Bull jam. Kellyville, near Tulsa, Oklahoma.

Western Heritage Show. Abilene, Texas.

Pasture near Datil, New Mexico.

Barry Clower. Goodnight, Texas.

Clarendon, Texas.

Bull awaiting rider at Dos Amigos. Odessa, Texas.

Boquillas crossing point over the Rio Grande, Big Bend, Texas.

Barry Clower. Sandy's, Texas.

Rhett Cauble. JA Ranch, Texas.

Rhett Cauble (left) and boys, Carrol-Jack Lewis (right), waiting for the fire to heat their branding irons.
This was the first branding that the boys, Brett, Billy and Bren, would do themselves. JA Ranch, Texas.

The Cauble boys wait to go to work.

John Merrow, windmill fixer. Clarendon, Texas.

Randy Davis. CS Ranch, New Mexico.

Saddle room. Haleakala Ranch, Maui, Hawaii.

Jack Craft. Abilene, Texas.

Jason Maddox (left), and friend. Bauxite, Arkansas.

Jason Maddox.

Jason Maddox at home. Bauxite, Arkansas.

The day begins. Cimarron River, Oklahoma.

Clover Stroud, who came from England to work on the JA Ranch, Texas.

Ricki Harper and Chelsi Johnson, passing time before Ricki gets on a bull. Odessa, Texas.

INMATES TAMED BY WILD HORSES

I've seen a few people breaking horses, or 'bending' as it's called. But when I was invited to the East Cañon Correctional Complex in Cañon City, Colorado, to witness inmates bending horses I was in for something of a surprise. Living in a world of overcrowded prisons, these men rose at dawn every day and made their way down to a stretch of land most ranchers would be proud to own.

The Bureau of Land Management (BLM) and the prison authorities started this programme after mountain dwellers complained to the BLM that the culling of wild mustangs was unacceptable. Today these magnificent horses are gathered and sold at a knock-down rate to the prison service. The inmates, who have five years' parole eligibility and are cleared for minimum security facilities, enter this programme of their own free will.

I watched as men who were jailed for gang murder learnt that there is something in nature that is stronger than they are. They came away with a strong sense of responsibility for the animals in their care and a great lesson in concentration and effort in a concerted task.

After each horse's 'bending', they are sold to people who want horses as pack animals or for general recreation and the BLM takes about $100 per horse sold.

One inmate I spoke with had become so involved with the programme that he had discovered what was missing in his life, and was convinced that on his release that he would go and work on a ranch.

I am not any sort of a judge of the man, but he looked pretty good with a horse. I wish him well on his journey for redemption.

Bill Craft. Texas Panhandle.

Henry Silva. Haleakala Ranch, Maui, Hawaii.

High up on the Haleakala Volcano.

From my mount. Hawaii.

Bell Ranch, New Mexico.

Texas Panhandle.

Paniolos (cowboys). Maui, Hawaii.

Round up at Bill Craft's. Texas.

Jack Craft, hot summer days. Texas.

Long drive. Bell Ranch, New Mexico.

Vincent Ranch, Kenton, Oklahoma.

Driving cattle across the Cimarron River, Oklahoma.

Father and daughter. BO-9 Ranch, just north of Phoenix, Arizona.

South pasture, Haleakala Ranch, Maui, Hawaii.

Chris Baldwin and Glen Souza. Haleakala Ranch, Maui, Hawaii.

Phil Fox. 6666 Ranch, Guthrie, Texas.

Henry Silva. Haleakala Ranch, Maui, Hawaii.

Heldorado Days. Tombstone, Arizona.

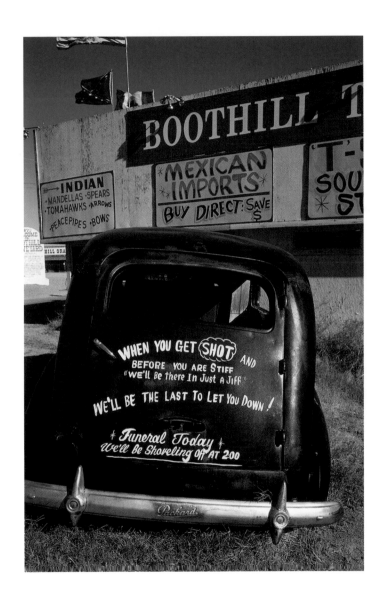

Boothill Cemetery, Tombstone.

I-40 west of Amarillo, Texas.

Canyon De Chelley, Arizona.

Near Wickeup, Arizona.

Gate latch. Texas.

Jim White. At home near Valentine, Texas.

John Means. Near Valentine, Texas.

Bill Evans, on the road to Valentine. Bill said, 'If the rain does not come in the next two weeks I'm finished.'

Roping practice. Western Heritage Show, Abilene, Texas.

Roper Vance. Adrian, Texas.

Jack Craft. Oaks Creek, Texas Panhandle.

Breaking the ice.

WINTER IN WIDE-OPEN WYOMING

February 1999. I found myself heading into sagebrush country in the Wyoming basin. The Dee Ranch is about twenty-five miles along a track that is as vicious as a bed of nails. 'At least three punctures a week on a Ford F250 pick-up,' I was assured was the norm by Greg Gardner. I'd be stranded, left to the mercy of the coyotes that roam these hills, if my tyres fell foul of the jagged road surface.

The Dee comprises three areas of ranch land, the Barclay Place, the Fuller Place, and the Dee. The Dee is high up on the Bridger Creek between the Copper Mountains and the Bighorns at about 6,000 feet.

The Dee itself is really only used during the summer, as the winters in Wyoming are harsh and the cattle are taken down to winter pastures. The main winter camp is the Barclay Place, which is home to the Gardners.

This land once comprised fifty-seven homesteads all working the land together, but slowly people moved on, and so the remaining families gradually acquired more land through marriage. Today the Dee Ranch comprises about 125,000 acres of deeded, BLM and federal land, about a third of which Greg, Barbara and the two boys Jason and James have to work come rain or shine.

One of the stories about the ranch concerns a man called Putney who lived here. He turned outlaw when he robbed a bank and stole money belonging to the Wyoming Stock Growers' Association. He claimed that the only reason that he robbed the bank was to get his own money back. The stock growers had rounded up some cattle, which included his, and then sold them. The stock growers claimed that as Putney had not registered his brand the cattle were fair game. Putney did not have the money to register his brand at a fee of $200. Gone are the days of robbing banks and waking up to find somebody else's horses in your corral and yours gone, but the battles with the BLM and other agencies continue.

The weekday routine on the ranch is fairly mundane. Up at 6 a.m., start the pick-up. The temperature outside is a cool −25 degrees. The boys go off to school. Barbara goes off to feed the horses, then she has some

Greg Gardner puts out hay on the Dee Ranch. Lysite, Wyoming.

The Gardner family, who work the Dee Ranch.

time to make phone calls and to do the paperwork for the ranch. The bank plays a major part of life at this time of year, the family need money to buy feed and cattle that will produce calves. A calf at birth is worth $300 in the bank.

Meanwhile, down at the Fuller Place day is becoming night and night day. Greg has been getting up at two-hour intervals to check his heifers, which are now calving.

'Eighteen last night . . . lost one, it died inside, and the poor bitch couldn't get it out, it took me two hours to help that lady . . . That's three hundred bucks I gotta to make elsewhere.'

The short walk from Greg's cabin to the heifers' corral is normally a chance to scare off wandering coyotes in search of one Greg's newborns for a meal. Tonight the 60 m.p.h. wind was carrying first rain, then just before dawn a couple of feet of snow.

'I was soaked through in minutes . . . That rain froze, and I couldn't open the door to the workshop, it was colder than a sonovabitch, but I gotta get the cows and their babies in. This is only the start, I've got three months of it.' All this before breakfast.

Today, Greg's going to spend some money. Barbara is taking care of the feed for the cattle on the various grazing pastures, which are all sagebrush. She has to load hay and a mix of hay and alfalfa, and put the pickup in drive at a crawl, jump on the back and fork it off as the pickup makes its way across the brush. Meanwhile Greg is off to the Jarvis Ranch where he's got to brand, load and pay for thirty-seven cows, almost all pregnant. At the end of a morning of jokes at everybody's expense, out comes the chequebook and bang goes $25,000.

'Mind you, English, they're fine-looking animals.'

Lunch is served at the Jarvis home, where stories are told of yesteryear. But also it's a good opportunity to catch up with local gossip and to discuss requirements for the up-coming season.

In the truck on the way back to the Fuller place Greg chuckles, 'You know that Jarvis, he's a crazy sonova. Don't go out with him, he'll get you in trouble.' The story is that one night at a bar in Shoshone, Mike Jarvis got so hungry he ate the fish in the fish tank, then went home for dinner.

'The thing out here is that you need to see people,

it's fine to talk on the phone or on the radio, but I can go days without seeing anybody.'

During the winter months Greg does a great deal of travelling around the ranch by pick-up on the maze of tracks that service some of the natural gas outlets that are dotted across the bottom of the Copper Mountains. It's easier then to go visit, have lunch, talk and move on to the next job.

'I was driving back from old man Fuller one afternoon when I saw this women on the track . . . she was so damn drunk she'd let her truck slide into the creek.'

'"Oh, please help . . . I'll get into so much trouble . . . it's not my truck, I borrowed it to get home."

'I helped her with a tow rope . . . she was a crazy woman and drunker than I've ever been.'

On the weekends Greg and Barbara have the help of their two identical twin sons, Jason and James, eighteen years old. Greg relies on the boys when there's lots to do, rather than hiring hands.

'I don't really want to hire hands because they don't know the ranch ways, I spend more time teaching them how to look after cattle than working them.'

The dilemma is will the boys, who want to live some of their lives away from the ranch, take over from Greg and Barbara when the time comes? I asked Greg if he had any advice.

'Don't hire no rodeo cowboy . . . Them sons ain't worth the powder to blow them to hell.'

The fact is that yes they will continue the tradition and yes they will travel and do all the things that young kids do, but they will also be there to help with the ranch work.

Greg Gardner, in the old bunkhouse.

Beef is good.